Greater Than a

I think the series is wonderful and beneficial for tourists to get information before visiting the city.
-Seckin Zumbul, Izmir Turkey

I am a world traveler who has read many trip guides but this one really made a difference for me. I would call it a heartfelt creation of a local guide expert instead of just a guide.
-Susy, Isla Holbox, Mexico

New to the area like me, this is a must have!
-Joe, Bloomington, USA

This is a good series that gets down to it when looking for things to do at your destination without having to read a novel for just a few ideas.
-Rachel, Monterey, USA

Good information to have to plan my trip to this destination.
-Pennie Farrell, Mexico

Aptly titled, you won't just be a tourist after reading this book. You'll be greater than a tourist!
-Alan Warner, Grand Rapids, USA

Thank you for a fantastic book.
-Don, Philadelphia, USA
Great ideas for a port day.
-Mary Martin USA

Stephen Floyd

Even though I only have three days to spend in San Miguel in an upcoming visit, I will use the author's suggestions to guide some of my time there. An easy read - with chapters named to guide me in directions I want to go.
-Robert Catapano, USA

Great insights from a local perspective! Useful information and a very good value!
-Sarah, USA

This series provides an in-depth experience through the eyes of a local. Reading these series will help you to travel the city in with confidence and it'll make your journey a unique one.
-Andrew Teoh, Ipoh, Malaysia

>TOURIST

GREATER THAN A TOURIST – FAIRBANKS ALASKA USA

50 Travel Tips from a Local

Stephen Floyd

Stephen Floyd

Greater Than a Tourist- Fairbanks Alaska Copyright © 2018 by CZYK Publishing LLC.
All Rights Reserved.

All rights reserved. No part of this book may be reproduced in any form or by any electronic or mechanical means including information storage and retrieval systems, without permission in writing from the author. The only exception is by a reviewer, who may quote short excerpts in a review.

Cover Image: United States Air Force photo by Senior Airman Joshua Strang - http://www.af.mil/weekinphotos/wipgallery.asp?week=97&idx=9

Edited by: Melanie Hawthorne

CZYK PUBLISHING

Greater Than a Tourist
Visit our website at www.GreaterThanaTourist.com

Lock Haven, PA
All rights reserved.

ISBN: 9781980752295

>TOURIST

Stephen Floyd

>TOURIST
50 TRAVEL TIPS FROM A LOCAL

>TOURIST

Stephen Floyd

BOOK DESCRIPTION

Are you excited about planning your next trip?

Do you want to try something new?

Would you like some guidance from a local?

If you answered yes to any of these questions, then this Greater Than a Tourist book is for you.

Greater Than a Tourist Fairbanks Alaska by Stephen Floyd offers the inside scoop on Fairbanks. Most travel books tell you how to travel like a tourist. Although there is nothing wrong with that, as part of the Greater Than a Tourist series, this book will give you travel tips from someone who has lived at your next travel destination.

In these pages, you will discover advice that will help you throughout your stay. This book will not tell you exact addresses or store hours but instead will give you excitement and knowledge from a local that you may not find in other smaller print travel books.

Travel like a local. Slow down, stay in one place, and get to know the people and the culture. By the time you finish this book, you will be eager and prepared to travel to your next destination.

>TOURIST

Stephen Floyd

TABLE OF CONTENTS

BOOK DESCRIPTION viii
TABLE OF CONTENTS x
DEDICATION 1
ABOUT THE AUTHOR 3
HOW TO USE THIS BOOK 5
FROM THE PUBLISHER 7
OUR STORY 9
WELCOME TO > TOURIST 11
INTRODUCTION 13
1. Getting There 16
2. Where To Stay 19
3. Camping 21
4. Transportation 23
5. When To Visit 25
6. Dress For Success 28
7. Winter Fun Abounds 30
8. Snow Types You May Encounter 31
9. Start Your Day With Coffee 33
10. Enjoy The Bike Paths, Parks And Green Spaces 35
11. Choosing Local Foods AND Restaurants 37
12. Try Some International Cuisine 39

>TOURIST

13. Visit A Museum 40
14. Check Out Pioneer Park 42
15. Ice Sculptures Abound In Winter 44
16. Experience Dog Mushing 45
17. Ice Skating Is For Everyone 47
18. Snowmachining Adventures Await 48
19. Snowshoe Rental Is Available 50
20. Try Cross-Country Skiing or Skijorning 52
21. Downhill Skiing Is Limited 55
22. Aurora Viewing Is Good In Fairbanks 56
23. Trap Lines Get You Into The Backcountry Quickly ...58
24. Fishing Is Fun No Matter The Season 60
25. Hot Springs 61
26. The Arctic Circle 63
27. Flights Are Mostly For Transportation 65
28. 4-Wheeling Is Not For The Weak-Kneed 67
29. Wildlife Is All Around You 68
30. Nightlife Is Musical In Fairbanks 71
31. Craft Beets, Local Breweries and Distilleries 72
32. Legal Cannabis Is A Thing 75
33. The Visitors Center Has Lots To Offer 77
34. Indigenous Experiences 79
35. History is Re-Written 81
36. Gold Mining Was The Life Blood 84
37. Fur Is Still A Thriving Industry 86

38. The Oil Industry Has Done Much For Fairbanks 88
39. Aircraft: A Vital Part Of History and Life....................90
40. Where Would Fairbanks Be Without The Military?....92
41. Santa Claus And North Pole 93
42. Farmers Markets And Craft Bazaars.............................94
43. Fun On The Water 96
44. Hiking Opportunities Are Everywhere 97
45. Phone Service, WiFi, And Internet..............................99
46. Postal Service...101
47. Shipping Meat Or Fish Back Home...........................102
48. Local Churches Are More Plentiful Than Bars 103
49. Camps And Retreat Centers.......................................105
50. Managing Time Is A Must...106
TOP REASONS TO BOOK THIS TRIP 108
> TOURIST GREATER THAN A TOURIST 110
> TOURIST GREATER THAN A TOURIST 113
NOTES..115

DEDICATION

This book is dedicated to my wife Erin and our seven children, whom we raised in Fairbanks: Zachary, David, Nicolas, Gabriel, Rachel, Kailyn & William. They enjoy Fairbanks as much as I do and inspire me daily to do what I can to make it a better place for the future.

Stephen Floyd

ABOUT THE AUTHOR

Stephen Floyd is a polyglot who grew up in Arizona, learning Spanish and French concurrently. After getting a Bachelor of Arts in Interdisciplinary Humanities, he enlisted in the U.S. Army and became an interrogator, learning Russian at the Defense Language Institute. When it became clear that peacekeepers would be needed to enforce the Dayton Accords in Bosnia, he was ordered to learn Serbo-Croatian and went to Bosnia for an entire year.

Upon returning from that crucial experience he and his wife Erin decided that he should get out of the Army and stay in Alaska, where they have now lived since arriving in 1994. Having worked as a Youth Pastor, a school bus driver and as a local radio announcer for 17 years, he got to know Fairbanks in a variety of ways, from the streets to the people to the nightlife and business environment. Stephen now works in a guest services position for Northern Alaska Tour Company where he actually gets to use his French, Spanish, Russian, Serbian, and fledgling Chinese. He also has a full studio in his basement, where he records audiobooks for Audible, iTunes, and Amazon.

Stephen Floyd

HOW TO USE THIS BOOK

The Greater Than a Tourist book series was written by someone who has lived in an area for over three months. The goal of this book is to help travelers either dream or experience different locations by providing opinions from a local. The author has made suggestions based on their own experiences. Please do your own research before traveling to the area in case the suggested places are unavailable.

Stephen Floyd

FROM THE PUBLISHER

Traveling can be one of the most important parts of a person's life. The anticipation and memories that you have are some of the best. As a publisher of the Greater Than a Tourist book series, as well as the popular 50 Things to Know book series, we strive to help you learn about new places, spark your imagination, and inspire you. Wherever you are and whatever you do I wish you safe, fun, and inspiring travel.

Lisa Rusczyk Ed. D.
CZYK Publishing

Stephen Floyd

OUR STORY

Traveling is a passion of the "Greater than a Tourist" series creator. Lisa studied abroad in college, and for their honeymoon Lisa and her husband toured Europe. During her travels to Malta, an older man tried to give her some advice based on his own experience living on the island since he was a young boy. She was not sure if she should talk to the stranger but was interested in his advice. When traveling to some places she was wary to talk to locals because she was afraid that they weren't being genuine. Through her travels, Lisa learned how much locals had to share with tourists. Lisa created the "Greater Than a Tourist" book series to help connect people with locals. A topic that locals are very passionate about sharing.

Stephen Floyd

>TOURIST

WELCOME TO
> TOURIST

Stephen Floyd

INTRODUCTION

> *"I would rather be ashes than dust! I would rather that my spark should burn out in a brilliant blaze than it should be stifled by dry-rot. I would rather be a superb meteor, every atom of me in magnificent glow, than a sleepy and permanent planet. The function of man is to live, not to exist. I shall not waste my days trying to prolong them. I shall use my time."*
>
> **—Jack London**

If you have ever read Jack London's stories about life in the Far North, you will understand my fascination with Alaska. *The Call of the Wild*, *White Fang*, and *To Build a Fire* caught my own imagination on fire when I was a child, so when I had the opportunity to list Alaska as a possible duty station when I was in the Army, I jumped at the chance. I have now been here since 1994 with no intention of leaving. We have raised our children here. We love living here.

Stephen Floyd

Life in Alaska is punctuated by the brevity of the Summer and the brutality of the Winter, so here in Fairbanks, we strive to use our time to its utmost. We do not waste our days trying to prolong them, but rather, we utilize every moment, making the most of each day. Whether we are outside playing in the phenomenal wilderness, or making our tiny house a cozy home.

When people come through Fairbanks on a tour, they often miss the little things that make life so enjoyable here. Hopefully, this book will give you a glimpse of what locals do for fun, and add to your experience as more than a tourist.

>TOURIST

1. GETTING THERE

The vast majority of people who visit Fairbanks get here by air, although you could come in by rail. If you are exceptionally adventurous, you could even travel up the Alcan by car. The fact is, Fairbanks is as far from the coast and the border as you can get in Alaska. Further North, South or West and you would be closer to the ocean, further East and you would be closer to the Canadian border. Fairbanks is, in a real sense, at the heart of Alaska geographically, and that is part of why the founders adopted the motto 'The Golden Heart City.'

Originally, people got to Fairbanks by steamboat, traveling on one of several large paddle wheels that brought gold-miners, trappers and entrepreneurs up the Yukon River to the Tanana River, then up to Fairbanks on the Chena. Although there is still a paddlewheel that takes tourists from the edge of town down the Chena, onto the Tanana and back as part of a historical ride, no commercial traffic goes any further up the river. The only exception is small river boats that take a few people at a time. Gone are the days of barges docking downtown, as 95 percent of all the food consumed in the entire state is shipped in through the port of Anchorage and then distributed by rail, truck or airplane.

Stephen Floyd

The Alaska Railroad runs from Seward through Anchorage, up to Denali National Park, and then on to its terminus in Fairbanks. Many cruise passengers take the train as part of their stay in Alaska. If you want to arrive in Fairbanks by rail, you would have to fly in or take a cruise ship to get to the railroad; there is no rail connection to Canada. Keep in mind, however, that the ride from Anchorage to Fairbanks is 11.5 hours. If you chose to arrive by air, the Fairbanks International airport has non-stop weekly flights to and from Europe, as well as numerous connections through Seattle. Even though commercial air travel is not as scenic as taking the train, it certainly is much quicker.

Lastly, if you have a passport and want to drive through Canada to get here, the roads into Fairbanks are kept clear of snow and are paved all the way from the border. Whether you take the Alaska Highway and come in through Tok, or arrive by ferry and drive up from Valdez or Anchorage, both routes are well prepared for you. Again, time is an issue, because a drive from Valdez or Tok will take a good 6-8 hours with few places to eat in between, and the trip from Anchorage to Fairbanks will run 7-9 hours, depending on how long you pause to look at Mount Denali (formerly McKinley). If you really want to see more of the state than most people get to, you could take the ferry up the Inside Passage, drive from Valdez over to

>TOURIST

Palmer (through Glenallen), duck down to Anchorage or even Seward and then take the train up to Fairbanks. This will add considerable time, days actually, to your travel before you even get to the Golden Heart City.

2. WHERE TO STAY

Once you arrive in Fairbanks, your choice for accommodation is as varied as your personal taste and level of comfort. From luxury suites in fancy hotels to rustic cabins, from bargain chain hotels to traditional bed and breakfast establishments. A simple search on Trivago pulls up 131 options, and that does not even include AirBnB! Many guests like to stay in the heart of downtown Fairbanks, where they can walk to numerous restaurants, gift shops, and museums. Others prefer to stay closer to the shopping district, where Walmart and Fred Meyer are nearby. If you want to be in a nice hotel right on the Chena River, or if you would like to experience waking up in a secluded cabin in the woods, every taste is covered.

I am the kind of traveler who usually prefers to skimp on the hotel room and spend more on food and experiences, but sometimes I need to be pampered and enjoy a five-star resort. Whichever end of the spectrum you gravitate towards, Fairbanks offers so many options that many visitors simply give up and let a travel agent plan it for them. In 1998, I saw this first hand when I worked at a local resort. My observation was that the independent travelers who planned their own trips or simply visited what they could when they could, seemed to enjoy themselves much more than those who were part of a package that rushed them around the state in a whirlwind of activity. There is more to see and do in Fairbanks than a simple overnight will allow. Seriously, you need at least five days in Fairbanks to see and do enough to get a real flavor of what the interior of Alaska is like. As you consider all the activities you want to do, think about what you would like to come back to for sleep. Is cost a factor? Plan for it. What about getting around? As you search the hotels, hostels, bed-and-breakfasts, cabins, and AirBnb, you may find several you would like to try. Why not try more than one?

3. CAMPING

If you are the kind of person who likes to 'rough it' by pitching a tent, there are dozens of campgrounds and RV parks in and around Fairbanks. From State Recreation areas to areas attached to hotels, you can find a place to pop up a

>TOURIST

tent or hook up an RV that is convenient, beautiful, and fun. Plus, no permit is required to pitch a tent on State land, so you can literally camp for free if you want to hike or take a canoe to an even more secluded spot.

I take my kids camping at least once a year, sometimes at a campground where we can have fire pits, well-maintained outhouses and water to pump, and sometimes out in the middle of nowhere, where I teach my kids (again) how to start a fire with one match using dead birch bark. The one rule we live by when we go camping is to leave the place cleaner than we found it, which is hard when you are camping where no one else has been for years or even decades!

Keep in mind that Alaska is wild, and the animals are dangerous. Whether you are in a campground or in the woods, the rule of thumb for any animal you encounter, moose, bear, wolf, or even porcupine, is to hold out your hand with your thumb up (just as though you were liking something on Facebook) and if you can see the animal around your thumb, you are too close. Most visitors get in trouble with moose because they do not consider them to be aggressive or dangerous like they might consider a bear. Do not make that mistake. Even though a moose will not eat you, both sexes have been known to stomp. Be especially wary of mother moose with babies and do not ever get between them!

That being said, although my head has been sniffed by a wolf (or a bear, I am not sure) through the wall of my tent, and although I have had moose and porcupines walk right up to the edge of my camp, I have never personally had a problem while camping, nor have my children. Usually, animals steer clear of larger campgrounds, but whether in the woods or right downtown, even a squirrel can cause trouble if you try to feed it or pet it.

4. TRANSPORTATION

Although we mentioned walking around downtown Fairbanks, the city itself is rather spread out and getting around can get expensive. In addition to taxis that run 24 hours a day, we now also have Lyft and Uber. In the summer months Fairbikes offers bicycles for rent through an app that allows you to find, rent, ride and return the bike, so you can use it as a self-guided tour or as a form of transportation (and exercise!).

Should you choose to rent a car to get around, most of the major companies are represented at the airport, but we also have several Turo cars now as well. In the winter months, you will want something with good winter tires, but four-wheel drive is not really necessary unless you plan to drive on the outskirts of town where the roads may not have been plowed. The rates vary depending on when you

>TOURIST

visit, there are peak rates that apply during the summer months and again during the peak aurora-viewing season. Do your research beforehand and find something that fits your personality as well as your skill level.

Keep in mind that if you find yourself wanting to drive up the Dalton Highway to the Arctic Circle, that there are only two rental agencies that will permit their vehicles to go on that road, Alaska Auto Rental and Arctic Outfitters. The primary reason why the other companies will not permit you to take their cars up the Haul Road is that if you break down there is no phone service, and even if you flag down a trucker, the towing expense can be astronomical. Arctic Outfitters sends their cars out with 2 spare tires and a CB radio (plus a satellite phone in the winter) and can also book you a room at the Yukon River, Coldfoot, and Deadhorse as part of the rental. For driving around town any rental car will do just fine, so you would not need the special outfitting done for the Dalton Highway.

I like to walk, even in the winter, getting around the one-way streets and cutting through parking lots makes travel easier downtown if you walk to your destination. We also have a number of bike paths to make life enjoyable in the summer, and the Borough does a good job of keeping them plowed in the winter. Enabling people to run, jog, to walk their dogs, or even bike year round. Keep in mind that when we get heavy snow, the roads are plowed before the sidewalks, so if you visit in the winter, you may want to plan on paying for a ride.

5. WHEN TO VISIT

Whether you choose to come during Golden Days, in July, or during the dead of Winter to see the auroras, you should definitely plan on making a separate trip to come in the opposite season too. No matter the weather, Fairbanks is a fun place. During the Summer solstice, you can enjoy the Midnight Sun Festival, a free 12-hour street fair on the Sunday closest to June 21st, featuring live musical performances, numerous local vendors with Alaska-made merchandise and food, plus a climbing wall and pony rides for the kids. That same week, you can participate in the Midnight Sun run, along with thousands of Fairbanksans, many dressed in silly costumes. It is a fund-raiser, but also a fun tradition that dates back to the early 80s. More people line the streets of the neighborhoods that the race winds through than those who actually run in it, and the entire atmosphere is a celebration of life under the Midnight Sun. On June 21st itself, you can catch the Midnight Sun Baseball game, a tradition that dates back to the earliest days of the city, where you can watch a baseball game that

>TOURIST

continues through the hour of midnight and never uses a single artificial light!

Later in the Summer, Fairbanks celebrates its founding with a week-long series of special events, including another street fair, the biggest parade in Alaska, comedy shows and people dressed in early 1900s garb, called Golden Days. Highlights include the River Regatta, where people build boats out of scraps, plastic, cardboard and duct tape and try to keep them afloat as they drift down the Chena River from the Barnette Street bridge to Pioneer Park. There's also the Rubber Duckie race, where people 'buy' a rubber duck and watch as thousands of them float down the river, with the 'winner' earning a large cash prize.

At the beginning of August, the Tanana Valley State Fair comes to town, complete with all the food, rides and booths common to most fairs. This is the time to see the giant cabbages grown in local gardens, view the 4H livestock and participate in classic games like watermelon eating, but most kids go to ride on the Midway. Locals see it as the unofficial start of Fall because it usually rains most days and starts to turn chilly at night. Because it finally begins to get dark at night, the end of the Fair features fireworks, which we usually miss out on for July 4th because of the near continuous daylight. For that matter, New Year's Eve is a big night for fireworks in Fairbanks for the same reason.

If you decide to come in Autumn, the middle of September is spectacular for the Fall colors. The birch trees explodes into yellow seas of gold, punctuated by the reds and oranges of the lower foliage. When you fly above the Arctic Circle during this time you will be amazed by the tundra's majestic hues. As lovely as it is, the season is excruciatingly short; I jokingly tell my friends that Fall is my favorite three days of the year. It is not uncommon to get snow in September, though it rarely stays on the ground more than a day or two. By the middle of October, however, the snow has set in and Winter has begun.

Do you like Winter? I do. But if you want to live in Fairbanks, you really need to love Winter. Whether you come up to view the Aurora or just to play in the snow, there is so much to do in the Winter that I almost made this book exclusively about things to do in Winter! It used to be that the visitor industry in Fairbanks virtually shut down during Winter, but now there are so many options that it might actually be hard to find a room around New Year's Eve, Chinese New Year, or Spring Break.

6. DRESS FOR SUCCESS

Whatever season you visit Fairbanks, we like to tell our guests to dress in layers. This will enable you to add a layer to get warmer or take a layer off to cool down. When I run

>TOURIST

at -65° I wear only four layers. The one closest to my body is polypro, a fabric that whisks moisture away from my skin. The next two layers are fluffy, to trap heat (often just a sweatshirt and sweatpants) and the outer layer is a simple windbreaker. I have seen many people, including my own mother, arrive in Fairbanks as if they are expecting to be put out on an ice floe in the middle of the Arctic Ocean. Unless you are planning to spend hours upon hours out in 40 below or colder, most of the time you spend here will be going from a warm hotel to a warm vehicle to a warm office or resort. If you are overdressed, you will overheat, and then you will get cold.

In the summertime, overheating is more likely, as we have seen temperatures up around 90° (32° C) and even though the sun never feels as hot as it does in the desert Southwest, it does bear down quite relentlessly in June and July. Dressing in layers in the summertime means being able to shed outer layers that you may have needed for a morning outing, or adding a light rain jacket in the evening.

Fashion is not something that Fairbanksans worry much about, especially since for so many months of the year, whatever you wear is covered up by a large coat. I have seen Carhartts worn to fancy dinners and crocs or overboots pass for footwear, depending on the weather. Wear what feels comfortable to you; we won't mind!

Keep in mind, there are a number of places that will gladly rent Winter gear to you if you think you need it, so there really is no need to buy anything special before you come. However, my experience has been that if you have a good coat and layers you can put on in between, you won't even need that.

7. WINTER FUN ABOUNDS

If you enjoy Winter at all, you will find Fairbanks a very fun place in the months of October through March. There is usually some snow on the ground throughout.. Although the snow here is a dry snow compared to what you may be accustomed to, you can still build snow forts and snow people and throw snowballs if you mix in a little water. Otherwise, most kids just throw handfuls of snow or tackle each other in the powder. When I was in the Army, all the newcomers to our unit were picked up and thrown headlong into a snowbank as a form of welcome.

If you like being active outdoors, there are a myriad of Winter activities to keep you busy. Snow angels are easy to make in the powdery precipitation we typically get in

>TOURIST

Fairbanks, but many people do not remember just how much fun it is to make them. Bring a child along who will get you to go out and play in the snow. Just remember to take along some water to mix in if you want to make snowballs. Otherwise, you may want to investigate dog mushing, snowmachining, snowshoeing, ice-skating and skiing.

8. SNOW TYPES YOU MAY ENCOUNTER

We already discussed the fact that the snow in Fairbanks is generally drier than the snow most people in the Lower 48 or Europe experience. That is a by-product of technically being in a desert. Because the temperatures are usually cooler, the snow forms smaller flakes that do not stick together as readily as the larger, wetter flakes with which most people make snowballs and snowmen.

There is a story often repeated that certain Alaskan peoples have numerous words for 'snow,' describing every variation seen in the vast expanse of the Northern wilderness. However, while everyone seems to know this anecdote in general terms, no one seems to know the specifics. The University of Alaska Fairbanks has published a recent study noting that this idea came into public discourse in the early 1900s, as a result of two articles written for magazines that gained national attention. The fact of the matter is though, that there are numerous languages represented across the Alaskan people, and the various types of snow remain vague.

Personally, I have noticed seven types: 1) a dry, sandy grain that will not stick to anything; 2) a powder that sticks to everything; 3) pellets that pile up and roll around like ball bearings; 4) a variation of the granular type that crunches like styrofoam under your feet; 5) big fluffy flakes; 6) wet, sticky goo; and 7) straight slush, also known as 'rotten' snow. Depending on the temperature and the humidity, you may encounter a variation or a combination of these types of snow during your Winter visit, but there is no guarantee that any will fall while you are here. The rule of thumb is that if you do not like snow, you will find Winter long and hard. If you enjoy it though, the time flies by too quickly.

9. START YOUR DAY WITH COFFEE

One of the first things you will notice about Fairbanks is our vast array of coffee shops. I am not talking about Starbucks, although we do have seven around town,

>TOURIST

including the airport and Fort Wainwright. No, in Fairbanks we have almost as many coffee shops as Paris, more maybe. If you are in a hurry, try one of the many coffee huts. From the seven Sunrise Bagel & Espresso stands to Mocha Dan's to Forget Me Not Espresso to Mojo to Go to Bucko's - you can actually drive right up to the window and get an espresso and a breakfast sandwich made fresh while you wait. These little stands are roughly the size of small photo stands I used to see when I was a kid, where you would drop off your film and pick up your developed pictures. There really is nothing like it anywhere in the world, having so many choices for good coffee on nearly every corner.

For another unique Alaskan coffee experience, you could try Alaska Coffee Roasters, North Pole Coffee Roasting Company, College Coffee House, River City Cafe & Espresso, McCafferty's Coffee House or Venue. Most of these establishments offer live music, art, and true barista skills. From the varieties of brewed coffees to the care taken by the barista to deliver an amazing latte, you will not regret any of these visits. Of course, many restaurants ALSO offer real espresso drinks, with Turkish coffee available at Pita Place and Sahara Hookah Lounge on

Stephen Floyd

College Road and Cuban coffee to be found at the Crepery on 2nd Avenue.

10. ENJOY THE BIKE PATHS, PARKS AND GREEN SPACES

Most of the bike paths in Fairbanks are paved rather than being made of concrete, and you will find them along the major roads as well as beside the river that runs through town. Conveniently, most of the paths connect a series of parks, so you could spend the day riding one of the Fairbikes from park to park, enjoying the sun and the sounds of the river as you do. Most people are impressed by the sheer number of parks in Fairbanks (over 50). The borough website has them all on a map, along with directions for ease of travel.

In the winter months, the bike paths are often cleared before the neighborhood streets, making it easy for walkers to get to work and for runners like me to get in a few miles without having to dodge cars. After a couple of heavy snowstorms, I have taken my cross-country skis on the bike paths before the workers got them cleared. That is another great way to enjoy the wintry conditions without complaint.

>TOURIST

From dog parks, Frisbee courses, and playgrounds for children, to benches next to the river, there are parks and green spaces in every neighborhood and you are cordially invited to join us in enjoying them. Some of the parks are better suited for Summer play; it is, after all, hard to use a slide or merry-go-round with three feet of snow on the equipment. Yet, even with Narnia-like conditions on every side, a nice walk in a park does the body and the soul a great deal of good.

11. CHOOSING LOCAL FOODS AND RESTAURANTS

Many people who visit Alaska ask where they can buy a moose steak. They cannot. It is illegal to sell moose meat. However, if you make friends with a local, you will probably be served moose or caribou because it is what we have in our freezers. Many restaurants serve reindeer sausage, which is as close as you can get, as the reindeer is the domesticated version of the caribou. And most convenience stores have some version of reindeer jerky sticks for you to try.

Although we have had chain restaurants in the past, besides fast food, you will not find a cookie-cutter approach in the Golden Heart City. All of our restaurants besides Denny's (the northernmost in the world, by the way) are unique, locally owned establishments. From the Pump House to Lavelle's Bistro to the Turtle Club, if you want prime rib, you will find it. Wolf Run, the Vallata, Pike's Landing, Chena's Alaskan Grill, Soapy Smith's Pioneer Restaurant, Lunch Caffe, Cookie Jar, Blue Roof Bistro and Sam's Sourdough Cafe all offer a mix of fine dining, casual dining, and diner food.

Truly, it is up to your taste buds and your budget, but you can eat really well here. If you are looking for a restaurant that offers Alaskana in all its regalia, try Soapy Smith's, Ivory Jacks or the Pump House. If it's more traditional fine dining you desire, Pike's Landing, Lavelle's, Zach's, Chena's or the Vallata is for you. For something more casual, the Banks Alehouse, Sam's, Cookie Jar, the Food Factory or Blue Roof will be right up your alley. And if you like international food, you have come to the right city.

12. TRY SOME INTERNATIONAL CUISINE

From Mexican food (Gallo's, El Dorado, Taco King) to Cuban and Caribbean food (Jazz Bistro), from Mediterranean fare (Eastern Treats, Pita Place, Bobby's

>TOURIST

Greek Restaurant) to Chinese cuisine (Lin's Asian Bistro, Bamboo Panda, Bei Jing Hot Pot), Fairbanks has a remarkably international restaurant scene. There are 17 Thai restaurants in the area, five Japanese, four Italian, three Korean and two Indian. 12 restaurants serve sushi, and most of the family-owned diners offer at least one international dish. Bring your appetite and your tongue's passport!

I have been very impressed by the ability of such a small town to support such a large variety of international cuisine, but with the great number of military personnel here, and their families, bringing in the international tastes they have acquired abroad, its really no surprise. That being said, it has been a topic of discussion among locals for years as to why exactly there are seventeen Thai restaurants in this little town in the far North. Any ideas?

13. VISIT A MUSEUM

Certainly, the crown jewel of our museum offerings here in Fairbanks is the University of Alaska's Museum of the North. With an extensive collection of Alaskan Native artifacts, dinosaur bones unearthed on the North Slope, historical pieces from the Pioneer days, mammoth tusks and other fossils - as well as taxidermy Alaskan animals, you can get a really good look at the way life used to be in

Stephen Floyd

Fairbanks. One of the most prized exhibits is 'Blue Babe,' a mummified ox who got caught in a bog thousands of years ago. In addition, the museum hosts rotating exhibits that highlight the research done at the University of Alaska Fairbanks, as well as special exhibits and the Rose Berry Alaska Art Gallery.

The Fairbanks Ice Museum allows visitors in the Summer to see the kind of ice sculptures that adorn the city in the Winter. Fountainhead Antique Auto Museum has some of Alaska's first automobiles and highlights the fearless and adventurous drivers who had no roads to drive them on. The Fairbanks Community Museum, Alaska House Art Gallery, and Two Street Gallery LLC are right downtown, and Pioneer Park has several others, including the Pioneer Air Museum, featuring unique aircraft. The Pioneer Museum houses relics of the early gold rush days, there's also the Tanana Valley Railroad Museum and a diorama inside the Riverboat SS Nenana (although the interior of the boat will now be closed to the public for safety reasons), all of which are only open in the Summer.

Lastly, don't forget the Children's Museum downtown, where kids are encouraged to get hands-on with every exhibit. From sensory experiences to giant building blocks, your kids will have a great time, and so will you.

14. CHECK OUT PIONEER PARK

Originally built in 1967 as 'Alaskland' to commemorate the purchase of Alaska from the Russians 100 years before, Pioneer Park is a collection of original log homes that once lined downtown streets, relocated onto a 44-acre plot along the Chena River. Every one of those log cabins has a local artisan's wares for sale, from Ulus to beadwork, snacks to ice creams. We already mentioned the museums, but part of the Railroad Museum is an actual working engine that circles the park, giving kids and those who are kids at heart a thrill as they enjoy the narrow gauge train ride! On special occasions, they bring out one of the original steam engines from the Tanana Valley line that has been restored. Careful, though, sometimes that can be scary for the little ones.

We locals use Pioneer Park for picnics and family outings, for company gatherings and community events, but we also like to take our kids, just to play. There is a good sized playground as well as an antique carousel, complete with wooden horses and the old organ music. Mini-golf can only be played in the summer, as the snow would interfere with the roll of the balls, and a recent addition is an interactive game that records your touch and movement with responding flashing lights.

The Alaska Salmon Bake offers all you can eat salmon, cod and prime rib, and the Harding car is a real piece of history- the railcar President Harding rode in when he traveled through Alaska to drive in the golden spike to denote the completion of the Alaska Railroad. From the Mining Valley to the Farthest North Square and Round Dance Center, there is more to do than meets the eye at Pioneer Park!

15. ICE SCULPTURES ABOUND IN WINTER

Most businesses hire aspiring artists to carve an ice sculpture or two during the Winter as a form of advertising and as a way to add to the festive atmosphere. North Pole (just 20 minutes from Fairbanks) offers an ice park around Christmas time called Christmas in Ice, and the World Ice

Art Championships are usually held in March at the Ice Park in Fairbanks. Whether you want to see some of the sculptures from the 100 artists from the more than 30 countries that send competitors, or just want to play on the ice slides and other child-friendly attractions at the Ice Park, it is usually open from February until the ice melts. Ice Alaska offers Ice Carving Classes as well if you would like to try it for yourself.

16. EXPERIENCE DOG MUSHING

Dog mushing has been called Alaska's state sport, and it certainly has a long history. It dates all the way back to the first people who used dogs to pull loads of food and supplies, and when the Russians arrived in Alaska, they found the locals using working dogs. After the American purchase, the pioneers and settlers used sleds and dogs, just as the established culture in the Alaskan frontier had done for generations. The famous 1925 serum run to Nome using 150 sled dogs and 20 mushers in five and a half days may be the inspiration for the modern Iditarod Sled Dog Race, but races had been held regularly in Alaska since 1907.

Although the basic terms are fairly universal, each musher may have his or her own commands for their dogs, and if you would like to run a team, you will have to spend an hour or two learning how to command these intelligent creatures with your voice alone. I personally own two huskies, and the older one was a retired lead dog from a team in the village of Ruby. He knows 144 commands, which is more than I know.

Whether you wish to experience a recreational ride with a competitive team, or simply use a musher's sled and dogs to reach a cabin for a secluded weekend in the wilderness, a number of local kennels offer mushing experiences. From a one-hour ride to a half-day of learning how to control a team of dogs, to a multi-day trip on the remotest trails, the best thing to do is investigate what you would like to experience and then ask people when you get here whom you should call. It seems everyone has at least one musher friend, but it is very hard to schedule in advance, as weather, trail conditions and personal commitments vary.

17. ICE SKATING IS FOR EVERYONE

While not everyone is a figure-skater or an Olympic racer, everyone who wants to strap on skates can do so in Fairbanks all year round. The Big Dipper Ice Arena offers a rink that is open to the public, though hours vary according to hockey practice and special events. The Rec Center on Fort Wainwright also has an ice rink that is open to the public. If you have your own skates, many of the elementary schools in Fairbanks have ice rinks that are kept clear of snow, and occasionally someone will clear off a section of the river ice to make room for public skating. The earliest days of Fairbanks saw public ice-skating on the river as a regular activity, but with the power plant pumping warm water back into the river, open water remains downstream of the plant for several miles.

Some of the cabins for rent around the Fairbanks area are near ponds that freeze over in the Winter and can offer ice-skating, and the Ice Park usually offers an ice rink that the public can use free of charge, complete with ice skates you can use while you are there.

18. SNOWMACHINING ADVENTURES AWAIT

If you have never experienced a snowmachine, you should at least once, to say you tried it. There are numerous guides who will take you on snowmachine adventures, often to see the Northern Lights, or simply to get out and enjoy the backcountry. From the adventurous thrill-seekers who will take you into deep powder to see what it is like to

Stephen Floyd

fly through snow clouds, to the slower-paced treks out to a remote cabin, there are snowmachine experiences for every skill level and budget.

Dressing for snowmachine travel is a little different than just wearing layers. You will want something that will breathe, so you do not overheat, but you also want something that will keep the wind off your skin and prevent you from getting frostbite or hypothermia. There are many places where you can buy all the gear you need, however, most snowmachine guides will provide you a loaner set or offer gear to rent. A helmet is a must; most serious injuries involving snowmachines focus on the head. You do not have to spend a lot unless you want to; even a simple bicycle helmet is better than nothing. The right gloves are also important because you want to keep your fingers warm and still be able to operate the throttle and brakes. Eye protection is more important than you may think; coming around a snowbank and brushing up against a twig at even 20 miles per hour can seriously damage an eye.

Although the dangers of snowmachining are numerous, if you listen to instruction and operate within your own skill and comfort level, you will have an amazing time and remain safe in the process. Most injuries result from poor-

>TOURIST

decision-making influenced by recreational drugs or alcohol. If you refrain while you are out in the snow, there will be plenty of time to partake once you reach your destination. Speed is also a factor in most accidents, coupled with unfamiliarity with the trail. Once again, the importance of going out with a guide who knows what he or she is doing and knows the trails where you are going is paramount to a successful trip. Do your research and choose wisely.

19. SNOWSHOE RENTAL IS AVAILABLE

One of the enduring images of the Far North is of a trapper, trudging through deep snow on snowshoes, dragging his furs behind him. While this still happens of course, all across the Interior of Alaska, the vast majority of snowshoe use now is purely recreational. Whether you are breaking trail or coming up the rear, pulling a sled with your gear in it, you are guaranteed to get a good work-out. Besides this, you will see views that cannot be seen from the road, get to hot springs that are not connected to a road system, or even walk across frozen rivers of landscapes that would not support the weight of a snowmachine or other form of travel. If you are a novice, classes are usually available at the spots that sell or rent snowshoes, but its really not that hard.

The first time I ever tried snowshoes, they were the military version that strapped onto 'bunny boots,' and I fell over several times in the deep snow. Eventually, I got good enough to go out front and break trail without falling once. As much as I have wanted to get a set of civilian snowshoes for myself, in the last twenty years of living here, I never have. If I were a trapper, or consistently went out into the backcountry in the Winter months, I would not hesitate to invest in a decent pair. For those who are just visiting, unless you want an expensive souvenir from your adventure, there is no reason to buy, when you can simply rent.

20. TRY CROSS-COUNTRY SKIING OR SKIJORNING

Like my snowshoe experience, the first time I ever strapped on cross-country skis, they were of the military variety that attached to my 'bunny boots.' There was quite a bit of falling down, especially since the skis were not well maintained and we only used them a couple of times. I compare learning to cross-country ski on those skis, to trying to ski by duck-taping two-by-fours to your boots. That being said, I learned to enjoy those outings and decided to get a set for myself when I left the service.

Like most outdoor equipment, you could easily spend thousands of dollars on items you will hardly ever use. I choose to shop at thrift stores and Play It Again Sports, a used sporting goods store that specializes in gently used items. I have found cross-country skis and boots for under $35 total, which you can easily spend in one rental session. That being said, you will not always find the used equipment you are looking for, or what you find may not be in your size.

Unlike downhill skiing, which relies on gravity to propel you forward, cross-country skiing requires you to propel yourself, so some instruction may be necessary if you have never tried it. Otherwise, get some skis and boots, get out there and give it a go! You will find groomed trails right in town, at Creamer's Field and at the borough's cross-country ski facility on Birch Hill. Each has its own pros and cons, and neither has a lodge where you could buy a beverage or a lunch like you find at most downhill ski resorts. I have seen more youngsters learning to cross-country ski at the borough facility, simply because it is maintained by Parks and Rec and the schools use it for their teams. I have seen more dogs at Creamer's Field, possibly because the trails there are mostly flat and skijorers can get good speeds there.

Stephen Floyd

What exactly is skijoring? I am glad you asked, because it is my favorite sport! Like dog mushing, the dog or dogs are positioned in front, wearing a pulling harness just like the Iditarod and Yukon Quest dogs wear. I typically take two dogs, as one, by himself, finds my weight hard to pull fast. I have seen skijor teams of up to four dogs, but that is bordering on sled-pulling capacity. The dogs are connected to a bungee, which is, in turn, connected to the harness that the person is wearing. My skijor harness can be adjusted if I loan it to someone, but typically, I tape the straps once I have them set so the dogs will not pull the harness off. Finally, the skijorer is wearing cross-country or skate skis and is pulled along by the dogs out front.

The dogs are usually retired sled dogs and the commands are the same, enabling the skijorer to control his dog(s) by voice alone. If your dog does not listen to you, you will get pulled wherever the dog wants to go instead of staying on the trail or getting to your destination. Right now I have an older, retired sled dog and a puppy from a mushing line (Buddy Streeper, famous for the Open North American Championship Sled Dog Races). The old dog listens to my commands and pulls the younger one into compliance so that the young one is now learning many of the 144 commands my older dog knows. If you want to try it, call a musher and inquire.

>TOURIST

Another fun place to skijor, without groomed trails, is the Chena River and Noyes Slough. Letting the dogs pull you through fresh powder is exhilarating! Two words of caution about that option: 1) watch out for thin ice, and 2) be aware of logs and rocks that the dogs may jump over easily, but which may snag your skis. Of course, you are welcome to skijor in the backcountry, if you want the work-out of breaking trail, but groomed trails are much easier, especially for the novice.

21. DOWNHILL SKIING IS LIMITED

Most people think of downhill skiing when they hear the word skiing, even though I usually mean cross-country when I refer to it. There are three downhill ski areas in the Fairbanks vicinity, Birch Hill, Moose Mountain and Skiland. The Birch Hill facility is part of the Army's MWR system, and although it is open to the public, you still have to go through the base security at the front gate in order to get there. The hill itself offers limited trails, but it does have a special inner-tube hill (for an additional charge) that pulls the riders up automatically.

Moose Mountain is Alaska's biggest downhill ski area with multiple trails for beginners and experts alike. Instead of a gondola type lift, the lift at Moose Mountain is a fleet of school buses that take skiers back up to the top. Lastly, Skiland offers full rentals, food, and tickets at the lodge, which operates Saturdays and Sundays through mid-April. They are also open nightly from 9 pm to 3 am for Aurora viewing for $30 per person.

22. AURORA VIEWING IS GOOD IN FAIRBANKS

If you think about the placement of the auroral band, it makes sense to come to Fairbanks to see the Northern Lights. If you are trying to view the aurora borealis in Europe, the places where they are most active are coastal areas where weather often interferes with your ability to see anything. From fog and rain, to snow or simply overcast skies, it is much rarer to see the lights in Europe than in North America. Although much of Canada is directly under the auroral band, there are few roads to get you there. This leaves Alaska, where you can drive yourself up to Coldfoot or take a tour locally near Fairbanks to see the aurora in a place where they are regularly seen.

Whether you take a tour or try to get yourself in a place to see the Aurora, keep in mind that one night alone may not be enough. Your chances of seeing the Lights go up

>TOURIST

80% if you spend a night up in Coldfoot, and up to 90% if you spend two. Northern Alaska Tour Company offers a variety of tours that get you into prime aurora viewing territory, including overnights at Coldfoot. They even offer a combination of flights/ground tours that take you above the Arctic Circle, and allow for aurora viewing on the way back. There are a number of other local guides who do evening tours near Fairbanks, but do your research. See what others have said on Trip Advisor. Find out how long your potential guide has been in business. Check how far North you will be going and how far away from the light pollution in Fairbanks.

Keep in mind that I live right in downtown Fairbanks, walked to work at 3 am for over a decade, and I have seen the aurora in every month that it gets dark, right in town. You improve your chances if you go farther North and away from the city lights, but the aurora borealis is a natural phenomenon and the only guarantee is that you are guaranteed not to see them if you don't look. Book a couple nights up North. Go on the tours. Go outside of your hotel and look to the skies between 11 pm and 3 am (when it is darkest). Do NOT expect to see them if you come between May and July. It simply is too light out.

Stephen Floyd

23. TRAP LINES GET YOU INTO THE BACKCOUNTRY QUICKLY

Unless you have a trapping license, I would not recommend setting up a trap line, as the penalties are harsh for those who do so illegally. If you know where to find a local trapper though, most would be happy to show you how they use responsible trapping methods and contribute to the North American fur trade. Trap lines are required to be clearly marked, with each individual trap labeled as to its owner. That way, if you happen to stumble across a trap line in your wanderings through the backcountry, you will know who to contact if you happen to unintentionally disturb one of them.

Ethical trappers do not want to snare people or their pets, but some activists have taken to unethically disrupting the fur industry by setting off traps or stealing pelts. Looking at traps and the animals in them is far different from trying to sabotage a person's livelihood, and I am certainly not suggesting you go out on a trap line to do anything but look. In fact, your best bet would be to go along with a trapper who can explain his methods and his motivations, while demonstrating the different techniques involved.

I am asked quite often where a person can buy Alaskan furs, and there are several stores in the Fairbanks area that sell both the furs and clothing made from fur - from beaver hats to mink coats. Every single one of those furs came from a trapper. Whether you simply want to know how the fur got to market, or you want to make a deal for a specific kind of fur product, ask a trapper!

24. FISHING IS FUN NO MATTER THE SEASON

Although I have been asked about ice fishing (where to go, how to rent the equipment, and how to get the license required), I have only been once myself. You drill a hole in the ice, let down a line and wait. If it is really cold, you do this while sitting in a hut on the ice, heated with a small fuel-burning space heater. On a good day, you may harvest a dozen trout, or you may end up sitting there staring at your fishing buddy for hours.

I prefer to go fishing in the summer when you are not confined to a hut and you are not miserably cold. Whether you like to fish for trout using bait or salmon using a fly rod, whether you would like to try for a monster pike using a lure or go after sheefish with a rubber decoy; there are numerous fishing opportunities in the Fairbanks area over the Summer.

25. HOT SPRINGS

There are numerous natural Hot Springs that dot the landscape in the Interior of Alaska, but most are not easily reached at all. Circle Hot Springs near Central, on the road to Circle on the Yukon River, had a resort that fell into disrepair over a decade ago. Although the locals occasionally clean the pool, most of the year it has long, grassy algae growing on every surface. The water does not smell bad, however, and even though you may be grossed out by the algae, the hot water does wonders for aching muscles at any time of year. There is no admission fee, as the resort is not open, but I would check with a local before jumping in, just to make sure things are cool. Some visitors do not clean up after themselves, which makes it harder for locals to trust people to use the Springs.

Chena Hot Springs is the most popular resort in the area, but the water smells highly sulfuric. The views of the aurora are amazing, and the amount of maintenance done around the pool and locker room area is impressive. The work done, however, is reflected in the price you pay for admission to the Hot Springs themselves. You do not have to have a room at the resort to buy admission for the day, but if you do have a room, you can soak to your heart's content and then sleep, without worrying about trying to drive the 56 miles back to Fairbanks before you can lie down. Over the years the resort has added a number of activities, including hiking, skiing, horse-back riding, dog mushing, flight-seeing excursions, snowmachine rides, bike rental, and even massages. There is also a year-round ice museum.

    Tolovana Hot Springs offers cabins and natural outdoor mineral hot springs, but visitors have to bring their own food and sleeping bags. To get here, you will have to hike or snowmachine in by trail or else take a small plane, as it is 45 air miles from Fairbanks and not road accessible.

Like so much of Alaska, Tolovana Hot Springs has no emergency communication or on-site personnel, so you do need to plan accordingly as this is a trip into the wilderness! If you do not have backcountry experience, this excursion is probably not for you, especially in the Winter.

Stephen Floyd

26. THE ARCTIC CIRCLE

A trip to Fairbanks will get you closer to the Arctic Circle than you have ever been, so making the extra effort to get all the way there is probably worth it, just so you can say you have done it. While there are a number of ways to get across the Circle, from renting a car to taking a flight, I would recommend a tour; that way you get a certificate from the company that serves as proof that you actually made it that far North, plus it removes a lot of the stress. You do not have to worry about safety or getting stranded, and you do not have to drive. Plus, you will learn more from the guide than you can possibly take in by reading roadside signage, primarily because there is so little of it!

As we previously discussed, Alaska Auto Rental and Arctic Outfitters are only two companies that rent vehicles that are equipped for travel on the Dalton Highway, but the prices reflect that extra attention to detail. The Dalton Highway itself is built on a raised gravel bed to protect the tundra, as the permafrost would melt otherwise. This puts your vehicle up at eye level with the tops of the trees on the sides of the road, and there is no hard shoulder to speak of. The soft shoulder will suck you in if you hit it and you will find yourself rolling off the raised highway. That is the biggest hazard of the Dalton, followed next by the hazards

>TOURIST

presented by other drivers. I strongly recommend leaving the driving to the professionals and going on a tour instead.

Whether you choose to travel North in a coach or elect to be flown up to Coldfoot and return via bus, there are many options to get you above the Arctic Circle, whether for a single day or on a multi-day package. Summertime brings travel all the way to the Arctic Ocean, if you are so inclined, as the road conditions permit it and the weather is better for flying through the Brooks Range. Do your research. There are many excursions to choose from, so look at which companies have been around the longest and have the best ratings on Trip Advisor. Do you want to go to Anaktuvuk Pass? Fort Yukon? Barrow (now Utqiaġvik)? Most of these places do not have lodging options, so you would be better off taking a one-day tour. Whatever you choose, remember that tourism is a distant second for most locals in these indigenous communities, and research before you travel will help you to be able to visit without disrupting their daily lives.

27. FLIGHTS ARE MOSTLY FOR TRANSPORTATION

As we just mentioned, you can fly into most villages. Without lodging or restaurants there though, if you just show up it would be like someone walking up to your back

Stephen Floyd

door and asking what amenities you have to offer. Another thing to keep in mind is that most of the airstrips in Alaska cannot accommodate large aircraft, so any flying you do is likely to be in Piper Navajo Chieftains or Cessna Caravans.

If you are interested in seeing the landscape, be aware that most of the flights you book will be weather dependent. If the pilot has to take you above the clouds to keep you safe, that is exactly what he will do! My first trip to Anaktuvuk was a mail run in September and the Fall colors were breathtaking, but the weather was inclement at Anaktuvuk Pass, so the pilot took us under the clouds at Bettles and followed the John River up to the Pass. Wow. With the river only 400 feet beneath us, canyon walls on either side, and a ceiling of 800 feet that obscured the tops of the ridges, I will never forget that flight! It was amazing! That may not be for you. Better, perhaps, to choose a flight that would be canceled if the weather dictated it. That would mean a change in your itinerary, but you know you would be safe.

Seeing the Alaskan pipeline from the air exposes the true nature of the engineering feat that it was, and gazing off into the distance at literally hundreds of miles of wilderness in every direction will give you the scope of how vast and untamed Alaska really is. Luckily, you are right on the edge of it in Fairbanks.

Once I flew to Fort Yukon with my then 14-year-old son, and he got to ride in the co-pilot's seat as the pilot took us over the White Mountains. As we climbed to 6500 feet, the pilot pointed out some Dall sheep on the side of Mount Schwatka. We counted 40 sets of very large spiral horns as we circled the extinct volcano. Then we went down to just 400 feet above the flats as we approached the Yukon River, just in case there was a moose to see. That is not a usual flight. Do not expect to see mind-blowing scenery and stunning displays of flora and fauna. Treat your flight as you would any leg of a journey, to get you to the next stop, but be prepared to enjoy the trip!

28. 4-WHEELING IS NOT FOR THE WEAK-KNEED

The first time I got on a four-wheeler, my friend took me right up the side of a perilously steep slope that I would have had trouble climbing on my own. I had to stand up on the machine and lean forward, into the hillside. He coached me all the way up, so I was not too concerned about getting hurt. Another time, my wife hired a guide to take us to a glacier on four-wheelers. They provided more instruction than my friend and it was a far less challenging ride. In the Fairbanks area there are no glaciers to visit, but there are guides who will accompany you on their own machine and others who will simply rent the equipment to you. If you go, go with a guide and get some instruction.

The experience itself is somewhere between exhilarating and terrifying. You will be able to go places that your legs alone could not carry you. Even better, because you do not need a road, even more locations open up before you to explore. Do not risk going without a helmet though, and listen to your instructor. They are there to keep you from getting crushed by the four-wheeler, should you lose control.

29. WILDLIFE IS ALL AROUND YOU

Many visitors ask where they can see moose, caribou or bears, and the answer might surprise you. You might see them anywhere! However, depending on the time of year, the foliage and the migration patterns might frustrate your efforts. First of all, most of the big animals stay clear of the roads because of the noise of the vehicles. However, if there is a lot of snow, the moose will use the roads to get around because it is easier for them than trudging through

>TOURIST

the deep stuff. When they come to a road, moose tend to hang out right at the edge of the treeline, which makes them hard to spot, and if they bolt into traffic you will not have much time to stop. Do not slam on your brakes. And do not swerve to avoid them. Just slow down as much as you can as quickly as you can. More wrecks are caused by cars going off the road because of moose than because of hitting them, and most moose-car collisions are caused by the car going too fast to begin with. If you do hit a moose, it will be fatal to the moose and your car will be totaled. So slow down.

I have had to stop my car and wait for a herd of caribou to get off the road when traveling between Fairbanks and Denali, again between Fairbanks and Delta Junction, and also between Fairbanks and Circle. Caribou migrate at different times of the year, depending on the herd, and you are much less likely to see a solitary animal than you are to see a dozen or more at a time. Hunting regulations restrict access to caribou when they are too near the roads, but when they do allow it, the harvest is quick. In fact, many Fairbanksans only hunt caribou when the regs allow road access.

Seeing bears is much harder. I was here for ten years before I finally saw one in the wild, but my wife saw several during her drives through Canada. I have had bears

Stephen Floyd

come through my camp on various trips; once a black bear tore apart my tent while I was out fishing for pike, so when we got back, we cleaned up and left instead of getting some sleep. Another time, when I was on the Yukon river hunting for moose, I woke up to the sound and touch of what I think was a bear smelling my head through the wall of my tent, although at the time I thought it was a wolf. When fishing with my boys at Minto's boat landing, we watched a black bear come down the shoreline straight toward us, then veer into the village at the last moment. Keep your eyes open!

    If you take a day trip to Denali National Park during the Summer, the odds are good that you will see all of the big animals in Alaska except bison, as they are nearer Delta Junction, and musk oxen, as they are found near Nome. However, the University's large mammal research station does have a number of musk oxen just outside of Fairbanks. If you want a longer trip, a visit down to Portage and the Alaska Wildlife Conservation Center is for you.

>TOURIST

30. NIGHTLIFE IS MUSICAL IN FAIRBANKS

Live music is abundant in Fairbanks, even on weeknights. Whether you want to hear a solo pianist playing in Lavelle's Bistro while you eat dinner, or a small ensemble doing jazz while you eat Cuban food at the Jazz Bistro on 4th. Many of the restaurants already mentioned also host small musical ensembles or solo artists, both as background and as the star attraction on weekends. Check the local paper on Thursday for the events happening over the weekend; there is always some sort of concert or live band playing somewhere in town. You will be pleasantly surprised by how many talented musicians we have!

There is only one 'real' movie theater in town, the Regal Goldstream 16. However, the old movie theater on Lacey Street has shown movies on special occasions and may again in the future. Also, the Blue Loon out by Ester, shows movies in their concert venue several nights each week. One of the perks of seeing a movie at the Blue Loon is that you can enjoy a beer while you watch.

Stephen Floyd

31. CRAFT BEETS, LOCAL BREWERIES AND DISTILLERIES

If you want to taste a variety of Alaskan beers, stouts, ales, and porters, you need only go to a local restaurant as most have several of the Alaskan breweries and craft beers on tap. One of my favorites is The Banks Alehouse, where they have nearly 40 beers on tap including ones from Kenai Brewing (Soldtona), Arkose Brewery (Palmer), Alaskan Brewing (Juneau), Kassik's Brewery (Kenai), Midnight Sun Brewing Co. (Anchorage), Silver Gulch (Fox, near Fairbanks) and Hoodoo Brewery (right in Fairbanks), as well as rotating guest breweries like Goose Island, 10 Barrel Brewing, Lagunitas Brewing & Angry Orchard.

Silver Gulch serves its own food (and was featured on Diner, Drive-ins and Dives with Guy Fieri on the Food Network). The building is a cool mix of ultra-modern and century-old, as the restaurant and brewery are built on the site of an old roadhouse and utilize many of the original structure's features. The food itself is unique, from the asiago dip to the black & bleu bison burger, but the real stars are the beers. Made with Fox Spring water, the Silver Gulch brews are making a name for themselves nationwide, but you can drink them at the source, right where they are bottled. Don't forget to bring a growler to refill, or buy one

>TOURIST

to take with you! In September, you will find much of Fairbanks celebrating Oktoberfest at Silver Gulch, if the moose hunting schedule permits.

Hoodoo Brewery does not sell food, but often has a local food truck parked outside the taproom. I find it amazing how many people can fit in the beer garden out front. Do not be discouraged by the crowds, the beer is worth the wait. This was the first place where I discovered the joy of refilling growlers. Instead of buying a new one each time, I rinse out the last one I emptied and bring it in for a full 64 ounces, paying only for the beer and not the packaging. Now there are several places, including Gavora's Fine Wines and the Brown Jug Liquor Store as well as the Fred Meyer on Old Steese, where you can fill a growler with any number of beers.

Fairbanks Distilling is an Artisan distillery where you can get locally produced potato vodka right in the old City Hall building downtown. Ursa Major is a small, independent distillery across from the Blue Loon in Ester, where they make spirits from barley grown in Delta Junction. And Hoarfrost Distilling, located on the other end of Fairbanks from HooDoo, makes vodka from barley and pure Alaska water. The laws governing serving drinks in distilleries have been changing faster than the tasting rooms have been able to keep up, so check before you go to see what you can expect.

32. LEGAL CANNABIS IS A THING

When I first arrived in Alaska over 20 years ago, my military command made it clear that although marijuana was 'legal' for Alaskans, it was still off-limits to soldiers. Turns out, it was not actually legal back then. A court ruling though on privacy surrounding an individual's possession of pot for private use, made it clear that having up to 2 ounces was not a crime. That changed in 2015 when Alaskans voted to 'legalize' cannabis and it can now be bought and sold openly in marijuana stores, where the state gets a share of the tax revenue. That being said, there is no 'legal' place to smoke it, and the federal government has promised to crack down on Alaska and the other states which have 'legalized' marijuana for recreational use.

Do not expect to find cannabis lounges or smoking rooms. Do not expect to be able to partake openly on the street or in your hotel. You can, however, expect to smell it. There are several legal grow operations around the Fairbanks area, with their own distinctive odors, and although it is technically not 'legal,' you will encounter individuals smoking weed in public. We do not have skunks in Alaska, just their odor.

And please, if you are military or hold a government job, do not assume that because it is 'legal' for Alaskans, that you can also participate. Government employees are bound by guidelines issued by the Office of Personnel Management, which has made it clear that marijuana is still considered an illegal drug by the federal government. That means that a government employee caught using or even possessing it will be charged with a crime. The military is even more clear, down to the section of the Uniform Code of Military Justice (UCMJ) that bans it: Article 112a, 10 U.S.C. 912a (Wrongful use, possession, et cetera of controlled substances). So there really is no time that you could partake, if you were so inclined.

I suggest that anyone thinking of coming to Alaska for legal cannabis use, and Fairbanks does seem to be the center of the nascent industry here, look at the law in your own state and your own personal conviction. If you would feel guilty or awkward, do not partake. There have already been moves to put the issue back on the ballot to re-criminalize it.

Stephen Floyd

33. THE VISITORS CENTER HAS LOTS TO OFFER

Like most local visitor centers, ours offers many brochures about local activities, including some that you would never find if you came to Fairbanks as part of a tour package. Do you want to do the same thing all the other visitors are doing, or would you like to try something unique? You can find everything from hot air balloon rides, to self-guided walking tours of the city.

The Morris Thompson Cultural & Visitors Center also has a walk-through exhibit about life in the Interior, complete with taxidermy animals including a wolf, a grizzly bear, and even a moose hiding in the dark. If you know where to look you cannot miss it, but if you do not know it's there you will walk right by, just like real moose. My kids enjoy the game of trying to find it! While you are there, try to notice all the amazing details in the supplies that most Alaskans call normal, if not for daily life, then certainly for when we are out fishing or hunting for days at a time. You can experience all the seasons of the year as you walk through.

Another aspect to the Center that is quite useful for those who might like to venture out into the wilder lands around Fairbanks, is the Fairbanks Alaska Public Lands Information Center. It is co-located inside the Morris

>TOURIST

Thompson Visitors Center. They can help you plan a trip to the backcountry, rent a public-use cabin, and learn more about the resources available. Many people who live here don't even know that you can rent a cabin in the woods! They also offer films about Denali, the Arctic & the Aurora, as well as programs on how to camp as a family and more. Discover Alaska's many parks and public lands in one easy stop.

34. INDIGENOUS EXPERIENCES

march

When I was a kid growing up in Arizona, I remember going to special events in Sedona and at the Grand Canyon. There, the local indigenous tribes wore traditional garb and performed dances for the tourists. That does not happen here in Fairbanks. What does happen is the World Eskimo-Indian Olympics during the third week in July, and the Festival of Native Arts at the beginning of March. These events are open to the public but are not free. There are also potlatch dances hosted by the Fairbanks Native Association that you may be invited to attend, but do not expect to just show up and watch.

If you drove to Minto, the only Native village on the road system in the Northern part of the state, you would be

65

driving right through someone's hometown. How would you feel if a person drove to your house and parked in front of your yard and started taking pictures? I have never had a problem going to Minto to fish, largely because I share my catch with the elders in the village. Many of the locals do not appreciate people dropping in unannounced, especially if they are coming to have 'an indigenous experience.'

Several tour companies do offer trips to Native villages, with corresponding tours from locals. Do your research before you arrive. The Northern Alaska Tour Company has evening flights during the Summer to both Fort Yukon and Anaktuvuk Pass, where you will have a tour from a local. However, the same 'no gawking' rule applies.

35. HISTORY IS RE-WRITTEN

Geographically, it does not make sense for Fairbanks to exist, as most cities are built at some sort of convergence. It may be where two rivers meet, or mountain ranges, or even trade routes - but there is usually a geographical sense to it that Fairbanks lacks. It is upriver from the convergence of the Tanana and Chena rivers, as far up as boats were able to travel before the Chena got too shallow.

The Fairbanks area had some Native presence before the arrival of the miners and trappers that came after

>TOURIST

Alaska was acquired from Russia by the United States, but there were no permanent settlements. Athabascan tribes had fish camps, berry-picking camps, hunting camps, and over-winter camps that moved around the area as the seasons dictated, but the actual founding of Fairbanks happened by accident.

E.T. Barnette was a con-man from Oregon who came to Alaska to start a new life. Outfitted with gear to start a trading post, he and his wife came up the Yukon River, and then up the Tanana. They hoped to reach Tanacross to start over in that booming area, due to reports of gold. Depending on your source, you will hear that the captain of the Lavelle Young, the steamboat Barnette hired to take him there, either ran aground on a sandbar; or that he simply had had enough and unceremoniously dumped them off on the banks of the Chena River. Whichever you believe, Barnette's wife had the same reaction mine did when she heard I was going to be stationed in Fairbanks: she sat down and cried.

A gold miner out in the hills above what is now Fox, Alaska, saw the smoke from the steamboat and made his way down to meet Barnette and trade some of the gold he had discovered for some badly needed supplies. Thus, the trading post Barnette wanted was established. Known for several years as Barnette's Cache, the city of Fairbanks was officially founded in 1903. Named after a Senator in Washington, D.C. Barnette was the first mayor, and apparently used city funds as he saw fit. He converted his store into the Masonic Temple in 1906, using public money and eventually cleaned out the account and left town with every last cent. Some things never change. Incidentally, the Masonic Temple was a landmark in downtown Fairbanks right up until March 17, 2018, when the roof collapsed after an impressive 80 inches of snow fell that season.

Going back to the convergence issue. Another town known as Chena, sprang up at the convergence of the Tanana and Chena rivers and was a competitor with Fairbanks for decades. Rail lines were built from Chena out to the mining town of Ester and connected with the lines from Chatanika and Fox, where the gold was actually being mined. Barnette had put word out that gold was found at Fairbanks, but that was not quite true. It was in those other towns, but Barnette wanted the business and Chena was taking some of it. At that point, a federal judge named Wickersham got into cahoots with Barnette, and they bribed the barge operators that brought supplies up the river to both Chena and Fairbanks. They offered to pay for everything the people in Chena had ordered, plus something for the trouble of bypassing that community on the way to the docks at Fairbanks.

>TOURIST

How would you feel if you had ordered a piano from the States, and watched it being barged up the river right past your dock, to someone else? The short story is that Barnette and Wickersham effectively starved out the people of Chena and after the flood of 1937, Chena did not rebuild. Everybody who lived at Chena either left the state or moved into Fairbanks. If you want to see the ruins of what remains of Chena, you can still see some of the old dock at the Tanana Wayside campground.

36. GOLD MINING WAS THE LIFE BLOOD

Those who came to Fairbanks seeking to get rich by mining gold, did not. Most of them froze to death, got sick or injured, or found a job working for a mining company. In fact, those who worked the dredges had a pretty good life. Excellent wages, with little to spend money on as room and board were usually included, meant that miners had money to spend in town. The red light district saw plenty of action, and the ones who really got rich in Fairbanks were the entrepreneurs who came up to sell goods and services to the miners.

Stephen Floyd

The hills around Fairbanks today still are littered with slag piles from the mines and dredges, and there are many artifacts from that era. Enough to fill numerous museums. You can spend days just visiting the mining sites and museums devoted to gold mining, if you are so inclined. At the start the gold was so plentiful, the earliest miners literally picked it up off the ground. Later on they turned to sluices, and then dredges. There is still gold out there and many Fairbanksans engage in gold panning as a weekend hobby. You can, too.

If you have never panned for gold, you might want to try one of the operations set up specifically for visitors to try their hand: Gold Dredge Number 8 and Gold Daughters both offer hands-on experiences without the expense of buying lots of equipment, or traveling out to a remote area. I went on a sheep hunt a couple of years ago that turned into a gold-panning trip when we could not reach the sheep due to swollen streams. One of the kids started sifting the mud and actually found a flake! Gold fever is real and you might just catch it if you are not careful.

>TOURIST

37. FUR IS STILL A THRIVING INDUSTRY

When the Russians first claimed Alaska, all they knew about were the fish and furs. If they had known about the gold and the oil, they might not have sold it to the Americans. As it is, they did not know what was in the Interior of Alaska, not even the people who lived there and called it home. When the fur trappers began to export large numbers of marten, mink, ermine, lynx, beaver, otter, and even wolverine, fox and wolf pelts, the hunting habits of the indigenous peoples changed. They began to reflect the trade in these fur-bearers, and not simply the animals they hunted for food for generations.

When the fur trade dropped off in importance, the number of trappers also declined but the industry continues to this day. You can still buy any of these pelts and more in Fairbanks today. From the Alaska Raw Fur Company, the Fur Factory, the Arctic Raw Fur Company, or Red Fox Fine Furs, you can pick up furs while you are in town if you want to. If you want to order a beaver hat or a mink coat, it will take considerably longer, but most stores in Fairbanks will ship inside the United States. Outside the States, you would be better off buying the pelts and taking them back home to be made into a coat or whatever you have in mind once you get there.

Other fur dealers include Suz Custom Furrier, Alaska Tannery LLC, and Fairbanks Fur Tannery, but if you are in town for the Open North American Championship Sled Dog Races, the Alaska Trappers Association holds an annual fur auction during the event, where you can buy amazing furs and benefit the trappers directly.

38. THE OIL INDUSTRY HAS DONE MUCH FOR FAIRBANKS

When oil was discovered in large quantities on the North Slope and development began in earnest, the resulting boom brought more infrastructure to Fairbanks than any previous boom. Expressways and traffic lights, apartment complexes and box stores all sprang up. The Alaska pipeline itself is a marvel of engineering that has not only stood the test of time, it has even surpassed its expected lifespan, and the jobs and money that came to the state of Alaska changed life in the Last Frontier forever.

Without the pipeline there would be no Dalton Highway, which would make travel to the Arctic Circle more difficult. Without the corresponding boom, the population of the state would have remained much smaller and there would not have been the hotels and restaurants that make Fairbanks so enjoyable for visitors.

While you are here a short trip to Fox, just a few minutes North of Fairbanks, will take you directly past a pipeline viewpoint. There you can get up close to the famous structure and take pictures, before heading to Silver Gulch Brewery for dinner and a pint of a local beer. Check out everything the oil industry has done for the community, including the birth of the Northern Alaska Environmental Center, which came about in an effort to balance development with conservation.

39. AIRCRAFT: A VITAL PART OF HISTORY AND LIFE

From the pioneers of aviation who brought the first Curtiss JN-4 Jenny to the Interior, to the first airline in Alaska (Wien Air), the Pioneer Air Museum inside Pioneer Park has fourteen aircraft. They also have some famous wreckage including part of Carl Ben Eielson's plane that he was flying when trying to rescue stranded passengers and one million dollars in furs stuck in the ice off Siberia in 1929, as well as part of Wiley Post's plane that he was flying when he and Will Rogers went down in 1935. From experimental airplanes to military craft, if you like aviation, you will find enough history in Fairbanks to keep you occupied for days.

When the first planes were introduced to Alaska, most travel was done by river in the Summer and by dogsled in Winter. The terrain in Alaska is simply not suitable for a road system beyond the meager highways we have now. From mountain ranges to tundra and swampy muskeg to thick forest, the cost of building roads has far outweighed the benefit to the few who might use them. Meanwhile, the use of aircraft made travel quick and much more affordable. Even today, the cost of a tank of gas to get to Anchorage from Fairbanks rivals the cost of a one-way ticket on a small plane to one of the villages in Alaska.

Whether you want to fly in a Piper Navajo Chieftain, a Cessna Caravan, or just want to look at the floatplanes on the pond, the East Ramp of the Fairbanks airport is lined with small planes and the small companies that operate them. Charter a flight-seeing tour, buy a ticket to an outlying village or find someone who offers fly-in fishing, and your aviation experience will be nearly complete. Just make sure you drive around the backside of the landing strip, between the East Ramp and the International Airport and take a look at the Fairchild C-119 Flying Boxcar. It's

>TOURIST

located in the tiny airplane graveyard near Everts Air Cargo. It is truly a unique craft!

40. WHERE WOULD FAIRBANKS BE WITHOUT THE MILITARY?

Between the gold rush and the oil boom, the U.S. military kept Fairbanks alive. All the planes that were sent to the Soviet Union through the Lend-Lease program of World War Two, came through Ladd Army Airfield (now Fort Wainwright). The DEW Line consisted of seven sites in Alaska and twenty-two in Canada, with Nike Hercules batteries stationed near Fairbanks during the Cold War (1946-1991). The motto for Fort Wainwright's infantry 'On the Line,' was still visible in the PX when I arrived in 1994. Eielson Air Force Base hosts the Red Flag exercises every year, with jets from around the world coming to Fairbanks to train in the country's largest air force range.

Since 9/11, the security posture has tightened up considerably, so you will not be able to drive on base like you could in years past. If you are still interested in seeing some of the historical and military sites though, a visitor's pass can be obtained with a simple background check.

Stephen Floyd

41. SANTA CLAUS AND NORTH POLE

The city of North Pole is just 15 miles from Fairbanks and began as a subdivision in the 1940s, where Army families from Ladd Army Airfield (now Fort Wainwright) and later, Air Force families from Eielson Air Force Base would buy houses. They'd often retire there as well. In 1953, the little community officially changed its name to North Pole in an attempt to attract toy makers who could honestly say their products were 'Made in North Pole'. They also built a SantaLand, like the soon to be completed Disneyland down in California.

Although the manufacturing never materialized, the spirit of Christmas did, and the Santa Claus House was born. Bring the kids to visit Santa all year round, and meet his reindeer. The Summer months feature a small train that gives rides around Santa's workshop and the Winter brings 'Christmas in Ice,' a Winter Festival, and so much more. Apart from the Christmas Spirit all year vibe, there is not a lot else in North Pole. So, if you are looking for a slightly quieter place to stay away from Fairbanks, without being in the hills, North Pole may be perfect for you.

42. FARMERS MARKETS AND CRAFT BAZAARS

The Farmers' Market is only open Wednesdays and Saturdays during the Summer, but I have seen smaller markets open throughout the year in various locales. There is the Arctic Market at the Tanana Valley State Fairgrounds, the Southside Community Farmer's Market at the J.P. Jones Center in South Fairbanks, and even a Monday evening outdoor marketplace at Golden Heart Plaza, right on the Chena River in downtown Fairbanks.

The Co-op Market Grocery & Deli sells local produce and eggs, and the Alaska Feed Company offers eggs and meats from local farmers, including hams from Delta Junction. Many of my friends sell eggs from their chickens to neighbors and co-workers, so if you like the idea of getting fresh eggs, local produce, and meats from small farms instead of giant corporate farms, this is easily achievable in Fairbanks. Even if you're on a short visit, you won't be disappointed!

There are numerous craft markets and bazaars at different times of the year so when you get here, ask your host what is going on while you stay here. It is nice to get away from the box stores to find foods, spices, tools, clothes, and more made by locals. As an entrepreneur myself, I like the idea of supporting other small businesses, especially those operated out of people's homes.

43. FUN ON THE WATER

Whether you want to rent a kayak, canoe or tp find someone with a jet ski or riverboat, during the Summer the Chena river comes alive with water sports. Many of the local gravel pits and lakes also follow-suit. There have been a number of river-based guides over the years, from those who offer hour-long tours, to those who will take you miles up a neighboring river to drop you off at a cabin for a few days. Do your research before you come and try to book something in advance because it is often hard to find any openings if you just show up.

Swimming in the Chena is not advised, as the water is cooler than you expect and the current can be swift. There are also a number of logs that can create jams that pose a hazard for both swimmers and boaters. If you want to swim, the nearby Chena Lakes has a swimming area, as do Tanana Lakes - but even in Summer the water temperature hovers between 35 and 45 degrees Fahrenheit. I prefer to boat or to wade in the warmer shallows.

>TOURIST

44. HIKING OPPORTUNITIES ARE EVERYWHERE

There are quite a few trails around Fairbanks for the hiking enthusiast. If you want a quiet, easy trail right through the middle of a waterfowl refuge, may I suggest Creamers Field? Originally a dairy, the acreage around Creamers Field began hosting large numbers of waterfowl way back in the 1930s when migrating geese and sandhill cranes would pause to take advantage of the freshly plowed fields. When the original owners decided to retire from the dairy business in 1966, local residents raised money to buy the dairy. They then got the state of Alaska to manage it, with more acreage added and the waterfowl refuge created in 1979. The trails are easy and there are several observation decks from which to enjoy the birds.

Birch Hill's cross-country ski paths become enjoyable hiking trails when the snow is gone, and there are multiple easy and medium difficulty trails in the hills around Fairbanks. A little online research will show you which trails are open to the public and how to get there from your housing accommodations. From powerline access to snowmachine trails, many places that look like well-traveled paths are actually restricted, so be sure to check with the locals before you start wandering into private property.

Further out of town, Angel Rocks is a relatively easy hike along the road to Chena Hot Springs. Grapefruit Rocks and Summit Trail to Wickersham Dome are considered hard. They are not for the casual hiker, only those with considerable experience. Keep in mind, that whenever you are outside of the populated areas bears can be a real consideration, so you will want to have bear spray and know how to use it.

45. PHONE SERVICE, WIFI, AND INTERNET

When I arrived in Fairbanks in 1994, there were still payphones in most stores, restaurants, and public places. With the advent of cell phones though that is no longer the case, and while you may have a good phone with an excellent national or international plan, you may not have service here in Fairbanks. Whatever phone you do have, when you get just a few miles outside of town you will not have any service whatsoever. This does not mean that you have to rent a satellite phone, but it is advisable if you are planning to go into the woods or up a river, even for a couple of days.